BODIES

ARE

COOL

by
Tyler
Feder

PUFFIN

For Coco and Spinny ♡

PUFFIN BOOKS
UK | USA | Canada | Ireland | Australia
India | New Zealand | South Africa

Puffin Books is part of the Penguin Random House group of companies whose addresses
can be found at global.penguinrandomhouse.com
www.penguin.co.uk   www.puffin.co.uk   www.ladybird.co.uk

006
First published in the United States of America by Dial Books for Young Readers,
an imprint of Penguin Random House LLC, 2021
Published in Great Britain by Puffin Books 2021
Text and illustration copyright © Tyler Feder, 2021
The moral right of the author/illustrator has been asserted

The authorized representative in the EEA is Penguin Random House Ireland,
Morrison Chambers, 32 Nassau Street, Dublin D02 YH68

A CIP catalogue record for this book is available from the British Library

ISBN: 978-0-241-51993-6

Design by Jennifer Kelly | Text hand-lettered by Tyler Feder

The art for this book was drawn digitally, with love, by a left hand with a crooked index finger.

All correspondence to: Puffin Books, Penguin Random House Children's
One Embassy Gardens, 8 Viaduct Gardens, London SW11 7BW

MIX
Paper | Supporting
responsible forestry
FSC® C018179
www.fsc.org

Big bodies, small bodies,
dancing, playing, happy bodies!

Look at all these different bodies!

Bodies are cool!

Lanky bodies, squat bodies,
tall, short, wide or narrow bodies,
somewhere-in-the-middle bodies.
Bodies are cool!

Round bodies, muscled bodies,
curvy curves and straight bodies,
jiggly-wiggly fat bodies.
Bodies are cool!

Leg hair, armpit hair,
fuzzy-lip-and-chin hair,
brows-meet-in-the-middle hair.
Bodies are cool!

Crooked faces, bump-nosed faces,
flat nose, full lips, gap-toothed faces,
stick-out ears and thin-lip faces.
Bodies are cool!

Freckled bodies, dotted bodies, rosy-patched or speckled bodies, dark-skin-swirled-with-light-skin bodies. Bodies are cool!

Hairy fingers, wrinkly fingers,
dimpled elbows, chubby fingers,
wobbly arms and stubby fingers.
Bodies are cool!

Soft tummies, saggy tummies,
flat or sticky-outy tummies,
innies, outies, pregnant tummies.
Bodies are cool!

Thick legs, scrawny legs,
knobby knees and long legs,
roll-up-to-the-table legs.
Bodies are cool!

Faint scars, bold scars,
stripes-from-getting-bigger scars,
marks-that-tell-a-story scars.
Bodies are cool!

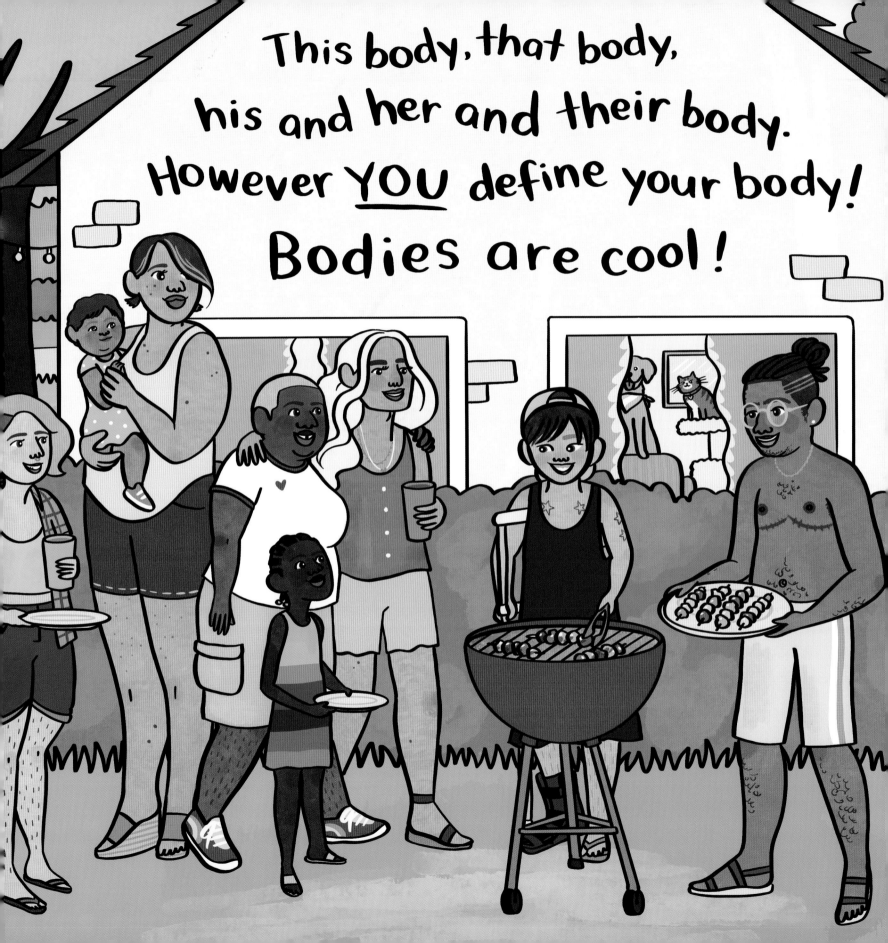

My body, your body,
every different kind of body!
All of them are good bodies!

BODIES ARE COOL!